Introducción a los padres

We Both Read es la primera serie de libros diseñada para invitar a padres e hijos a compartir la lectura de un cuento, por turnos y en voz alta. Esta "lectura compartida" —que se ha desarrollado en conjunto con especialistas en primeras lecturas— invita a los padres a leer los textos más complejos en la página de la izquierda. Luego, les toca a los niños leer las páginas de la derecha, que contienen textos más sencillos, escritos específicamente para primeros lectores.

Leer en voz alta es una de las actividades más importantes que los padres comparten con sus hijos para ayudarlos a desarrollar la lectura. Sin embargo, *We Both Read* no es solo leerle *a* un niño, sino que les permite a los padres leer *con* el niño. *We Both Read* es más poderoso y efectivo porque combina dos elementos claves del aprendizaje: "demostración" (el padre lee) y "aplicación" (el niño lee). El resultado no es solo que el niño aprende a leer más rápido, ¡sino que ambos disfrutan y se enriquecen con esta experiencia!

Sería más útil si usted lee el libro completo y en voz alta la primera vez, y luego invita a su niño a participar en una segunda lectura. En algunos libros, las palabras más difíciles se presentan por primera vez en **negritas** en el texto del padre. Señalar o conversar sobre estas palabras ayudará a su niño a familiarizarse con estas y a ampliar su vocabulario. También notará que el ícono "lee el padre" ☺ precede el texto del padre y el ícono de "lee el niño" ☺ precede el texto del niño.

Lo invitamos a compartir y a relacionarse con su niño mientras leen el libro juntos. Si su hijo tiene dificultad, usted puede mencionar algunas cosas que lo ayuden. "Decir cada sonido" es bueno, pero puede que esto no funcione con todas las palabras. Los niños pueden hallar pistas en las palabras del cuento, en el contexto de las oraciones e incluso de las imágenes. Algunos cuentos incluyen patrones y rimas que los ayudarán. También le podría ser útil a su niño tocar las palabras con su dedo mientras leen para conectar mejor las palabras habladas con las palabras impresas.

¡Al compartir los libros de *We Both Read*, usted y su hijo vivirán juntos la fascinante aventura de la lectura! Es una manera divertida y fácil de animar y ayudar a su niño a leer —¡y una maravillosa manera de preparar a su niño para disfrutar de la lectura durante toda su vida!

WE BOTH READ®

Parent's Introduction

We Both Read is the first series of books designed to invite parents and children to share the reading of a story by taking turns reading aloud. This "shared reading" innovation, which was developed with reading education specialists, invites parents to read the more complex text and storyline on the left-hand pages. Then children can be encouraged to read the right-hand pages, which feature less complex text and storyline, specifically written for the beginning reader.

Reading aloud is one of the most important activities parents can share with their child to assist in his or her reading development. However, *We Both Read* goes beyond reading *to* a child and allows parents to share the reading *with* a child. *We Both Read* is so powerful and effective because it combines two key elements in learning: "modeling" (the parent reads) and "doing" (the child reads). The result is not only faster reading development for the child but a much more enjoyable and enriching experience for both!

You may find it helpful to read the entire book aloud yourself the first time, then invite your child to participate in the second reading. In some books, a few more difficult words will first be introduced in the parent's text, distinguished with **bold lettering**. Pointing out, and even discussing, these words will help familiarize your child with them and help to build your child's vocabulary. Also, note that a "talking parent" icon ⊙ precedes the parent's text and a "talking child" icon ⊙ precedes the child's text.

We encourage you to share and interact with your child as you read the book together. If your child is having difficulty, you might want to mention a few things to help him or her. "Sounding out" is good, but it will not work with all words. Children can pick up clues about the words they are reading from the story, the context of the sentence, or even the pictures. Some stories have rhyming patterns that might help. It might also help them to touch the words with their finger as they read, to better connect the spoken words and the printed words.

Sharing the *We Both Read* books together will engage you and your child in an interactive adventure in reading! It is a fun and easy way to encourage and help your child to read—and a wonderful way to start your child off on a lifetime of reading enjoyment!

About Bats
Acerca de los murciélagos
A We Both Read® Book

---

*With special thanks to Alicia Goode at the California Academy of Sciences
for her review and recommendations on the material in this book*

Text Copyright © 2014 by Sindy McKay
Illustrations Copyright © 2014 by Wendy Smith
Use of photographs on pages 11, 32, and 38-39 provided by National Geographic.
Use of all other photographs in this book provided by Dreamstime and Fotosearch.
Editorial and Production Services by Cambridge BrickHouse, Inc.
Spanish translation © 2014 by Treasure Bay, Inc.
All rights reserved

Published by Treasure Bay, Inc.
P.O. Box 119
Novato, CA 94948 USA

Printed in Singapore

Library of Congress Catalog Card Number: 2012955733

Paperback ISBN: 978-1-60115-060-8

We Both Read® Books
Patent No. 5,957,693

Visit us online at:
www.WeBothRead.com

PR-11-13

WE BOTH READ®

About Bats
Acerca de los murciélagos

By Sindy McKay
Translated by Yanitzia Canetti
With illustrations by Wendy Smith

TREASURE BAY

⚬ Meet Brownie. **She** was born just six weeks ago. **She** can already take care of herself.

*Conoce a Chocolatina. Nació hace solo seis semanas. **Ella** ya puede cuidarse sola.*

👓 **She** is a bat.

Ella es un murciélago.

Some people think bats are birds, but they are mammals. You are a mammal too. So is a dog. What else is a mammal?

Algunas personas piensan que los murciélagos son aves, pero son mamíferos. Tú también eres un mamífero. ¡Y el perro! ¿Quién más es un mamífero?

A cat!

¡El gato!

Why do people think bats are birds? Maybe it's because they have wings and they can **fly**.

*¿Por qué las personas creen que los murciélagos son pájaros? Tal vez es porque ellos tienen alas y pueden **volar**.*

She can **fly**.

*Ella puede **volar**.*

During the summer, Brownie lives under the roof of a barn. She lives there with many other mother bats and babies.

Durante el verano, Chocolatina vive bajo el techo de un granero. Ella vive allí con otras madres murciélagos y sus bebés.

It is hot.

Hace calor.

In the winter, it gets cold. Brownie and other bats fly south to hibernate, or "sleep," in a cave. In the cave, it is not **too** cold and . . .

*En invierno, hace frío. Chocolatina y otros murciélagos vuelan hacia el sur a hibernar, o a "dormir" en una caverna. La caverna no es ni **muy** fría . . .*

...not **too** hot.

...ni **_muy_** caliente.

Brownie wakes up in the spring. She flies back to the same barn where she was born. All grown up now, she has a baby of her own.

Chocolatina despierta en primavera. Ella regresa al mismo granero donde nació. Ahora que es adulta, ella tiene su propio bebé.

 It is a pup.

Esta es una cría.

Brownie is one kind of bat. There are many others. This is a Malayan flying fox. When he spreads his wings, he is about six feet wide.

Chocolatina pertenece a un tipo de murciélago. Hay muchos otros. Este es un zorro volador malayo. Cuando extiende sus alas, alcanza unos seis pies de ancho.

He is big.

Él es grande.

This is a Kitti's hog-nosed bat. He is sometimes called the bumblebee bat. Can you guess why?

Este es un pequeño murciélago nariz de cerdo de Kitti. A veces se le llama murciélago abejorro. ¿Puedes adivinar por qué?

He is not big.

Él no es grande.

Brownie is a type of bat called a little brown bat. When she spreads her wings, she is about ten inches wide.

Chocolatina pertenece a un tipo llamado pequeño murciélago marrón. Cuando extiende sus alas, alcanza unas 10 pulgadas de ancho.

Is she big?

¿Ella es grande?

19

Most bats are nocturnal. This means they sleep in the day and come out at night. That makes some people think bats like Brownie are blind, but she is not.

La mayoría de los murciélagos son nocturnos. O sea, duermen de día y salen de noche. Algunos piensan que los murciélagos como Chocolatina son ciegos, pero no es cierto.

She can see.

Ella puede ver.

Brownie comes out at night to hunt for food. She **eats** moths, wasps, beetles, gnats, mosquitoes, midges, and flies.

*Chocolatina sale de noche a cazar para comer. Ella **come** polillas, avispas, escarabajos, jejenes, mosquitos y moscas.*

She **eats** bugs.

*Ella **come** insectos.*

Brownie catches her dinner using echolocation. She sends out a noise. It bounces off a bug and comes back to her **ears**. That tells her where the bug is.

*Chocolatina caza usando ecolocalización. Ella lanza un sonido. Este rebota contra el insecto y regresa a sus **orejas**. Así ella sabe dónde está el insecto.*

She has big **ears**!

*¡Ella tiene **orejas** grandes!*

Insects are Brownie's favorite food, but some bats eat other things. Flying fox bats fly off at night to eat fruit from **trees**. During the day, they often sleep hanging upside down . . .

*Los insectos son el alimento favorito de Chocola-tina, pero hay murciélagos que comen otras cosas. El zorro volador sale de noche a comer frutas en los **árboles**. De día, duerme colgado de cabeza . . .*

. . . in the **trees**.

. . . *en los **árboles**.*

The California leaf-nosed bat eats large insects like crickets, grasshoppers, and even caterpillars. **Some** bats eat lizards, frogs, birds, and rodents.

*El murciélago nariz de hoja, de California, come grandes cantidades de insectos como grillos, saltamontes e inclusive, orugas. **Algunos** comen lagartos, ranas, pájaros y roedores.*

Some eat fish.

Algunos comen peces.

Some bats do not eat at all. Vampire bats drink their meals. They bite and drink blood from other animals. They only take a little bit of blood at a time from animals like birds and deer . . .

Algunos murciélagos no comen. Los murciélagos vampiros toman sus alimentos. Ellos muerden y le chupan la sangre a otros animales. Solo toman pequeños sorbos de sangre cada vez, de aves, ciervos . . .

 . . . and goats.

. . . y cabras.

After Brownie finishes feeding on insects at night, she heads back to her home to rest and sleep. Bats usually sleep hanging upside down by their **feet**. Head down . . .

Después que Chocolatina termina de comer por la noche, se dirige a su casa a descansar y dormir. Los murciélagos duermen colgados por sus patas, de cabeza. Cabeza abajo . . .

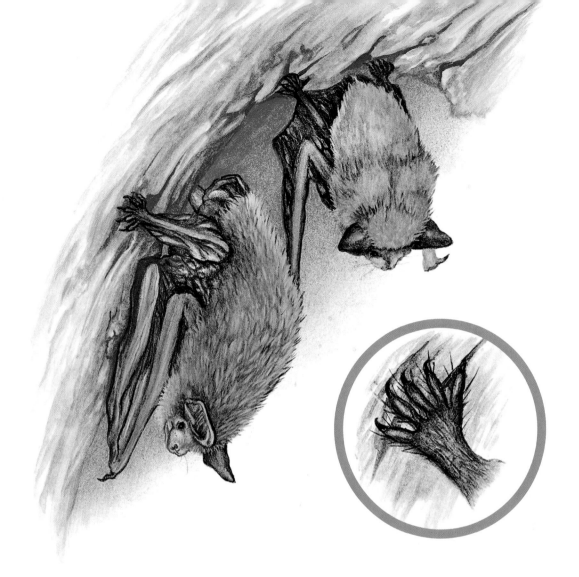

. . . **feet** up!

. . . *¡patas arriba!*

Most farmers like bats like Brownie. Bats help keep mosquitoes and other insects out of our orchards, fields, and gardens.

La mayoría de los granjeros quieren a Chocolatina. Los murciélagos eliminan los mosquitos y otros insectos de los huertos, jardines y campos de cultivo.

Bats help us.

Los murciélagos nos ayudan.

Some people even build a special house that bats **like** so that bats will live near them.

Brownie and her family . . .

*Algunas personas construyen una casa especial que le **gusta** a los murciélagos para que estos vivan cerca.*

A Chocolatina y su familia . . .

 . . . **like** it!

. . . ¡les ***gusta*** esta!

Wrinkled-lipped bats exiting a cave at dusk

Of course, not everyone likes bats. Maybe that's because they never learned about bats. Now you can explain to them how interesting and helpful bats can be. You may even say, . . .

Claro, no a todas las personas les gustan los murciélagos. Tal vez porque no saben nada sobre ellos. Ahora tú puedes explicarles lo interesantes y útiles que estos pueden ser. Podrías decirles . . .

 . . ."I like bats!"

. . ."¡Me gustan los murciélagos!".

FUN FACTS ABOUT BATS
DATOS CURIOSOS SOBRE LOS MURCIÉLAGOS

They live on every continent except Antarctica.

Viven en todos los continentes excepto en la Antártica.

They are the only mammals that can fly.

Son los únicos mamíferos que pueden volar.

They have four fingers and a thumb. The thumb is a small, hook-like nail at the top of the wing. It is used for clinging and climbing.

Tienen cuatro dedos y un pulgar. El pulgar es una uña pequeña en forma de gancho en la punta de las alas. Lo usan para colgarse y trepar.

Most are nocturnal. This means they sleep during the day and come out at night.

La mayoría son nocturnos. Duermen de día y salen de noche.

They usually have only one baby at a time.

Generalmente solo tienen una cría a la vez.

The Malaysian flying fox is the world's biggest bat. Kitti's hog-nosed bat is the world's smallest bat.

El zorro volador de Malasia es el más grande del mundo. El murciélago nariz de cerdo de Kitti es el más pequeño.

If you liked **About Bats,** here is another
We Both Read® Book you are sure to enjoy!

*Si te gustó leer **Acerca de los murciélagos,** ¡seguramente
disfrutarás al leer este otro libro de la serie We Both Read®!*

This nonfiction book for very beginning readers uses a touch of humor as it shows how different animals sleep. From pigs to puppies to penguins, the book offers glimpses of animals as they live, play, and sleep. In the end, the book even has the readers talking about falling asleep themselves! Rhymes and repeating text help make the reading fun and easy for the child.

Este libro de no-ficción para primeros lectores muestra las diferentes formas de dormir de los animales con un tono humorístico. Este da una visión sobre cómo viven, juegan y duermen diferentes animales, desde los cerdos hasta los cachorros y los pingüinos. Al final, el libro hace que los lectores hablen sobre cómo duermen ellos mismos. Las rimas y la repetición hacen la lectura más fácil y divertida para el niño.

To see all the We Both Read® books that are available,
just go online to **www.WeBothRead.com.**

*Para ver todos los libros disponibles de la serie We Both Read®,
visita nuestra página web:* **www.WeBothRead.com.**